OSCAR'S BRIDGE TO READING BOOK

Featuring Jim Henson's Sesame Street Muppets

Children's Television Workshop

Author

Katrin Tiitsman

Illustrators

Tom Brannon

Mary Grace Eubank

Jody Taylor

Oxford University Press

1985

Oxford University Press

200 Madison Avenue
New York, NY 10016 USA

Walton Street
Oxford OX2 6DP England

OXFORD is a trademark of
Oxford University Press.

Library of Congress Cataloging in
Publication Data

Tiitsman, Katrin.
    Oscar's bridge to reading book.

    (Open Sesame)
    Summary: The second book in this
ESL series for non-English speaking
children is designed to prepare students
to read in English with emphasis on
identifying letters of the alphabet with
the basic consonant and vowel sounds.
    1. English language—Text-books for
foreign speakers—Juvenile literature.
[1. English language—Textbooks for
foreign speakers] I. Brannon, Tom, ill.
II. Eubank, Mary Grace, ill. III. Taylor,
Jody, ill.   IV. Children's Television
Workshop. V. Title. VI. Series.
PE1128.T5   1985   428.3′4   84-16522
ISBN 0-19-434171-2

The publisher would like to thank Tom
Cooke for permission to reproduce *Meet
the Muppets*.

Printing (last digit): 9 8 7 6 5 4 3 2 1

Printed in Hong Kong

PREFACE

Oscar's Bridge to Reading Book
prepares elementary school children
to begin reading in English.
Students are taught to identify
letters with basic consonant and
vowel sounds, and to read vocab-
ulary that was first introduced
orally in Open Sesame Stage A
through a carefully planned readi-
ness approach. The illustrations
encourage imaginative thinking and
are based on topics particularly
suitable for children, such as
birthdays, toys, and animals.

The full-color Student Book is
directly integrated with the Activity
Book, in which students start
writing. For page 1–27, the Student
Book is used before the Activity
Book. For pages 28–44, the Activity
Book is used before the Student
Book. The order is indicated on
each Student Book page.

Other components at this level
include a Teacher's Book, an Activity
Book, a Cassette, and Picture Cards.

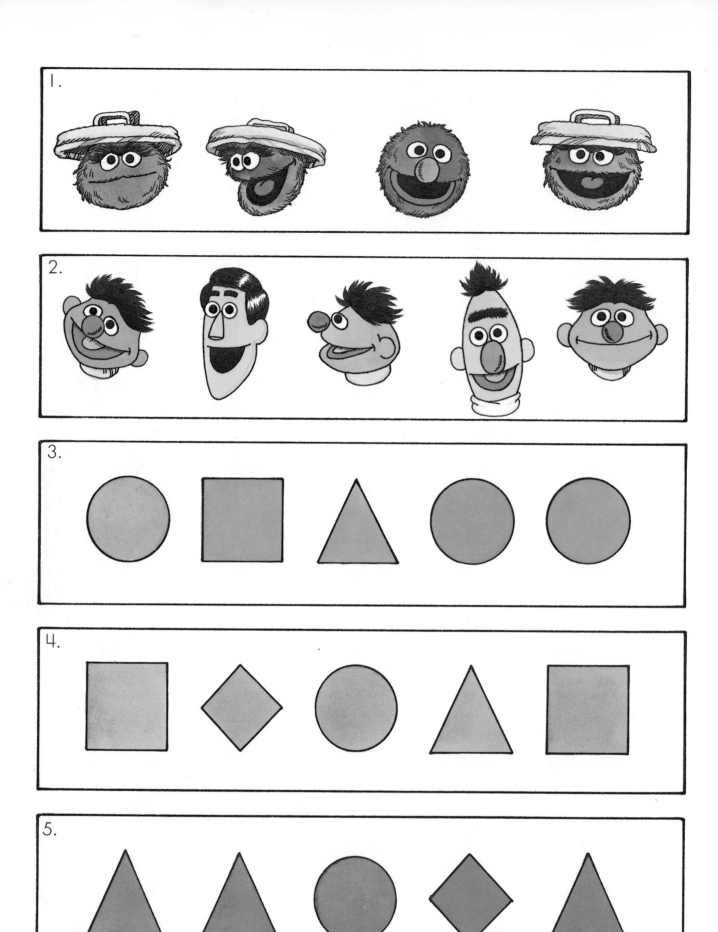

1.

2.

3.

4.

5.

⟶ Activity Book 2

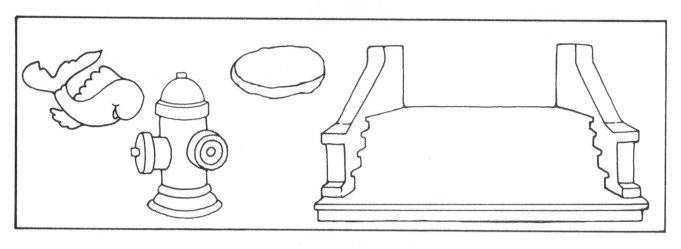

I	ME	I
IT	IT	FACE
MAN	MAN	OPEN
NINE	NO	NINE
RAN	RAN	NAPKINS
garden	go	garden
delicious	dog	delicious

⟶ Activity Book 23–28

Sammy the Snake

Malcolm Monster

⟶ Activity Book 30

Five Fat Fish

Jump in June

→ Activity Book 32

A Little Lamb

Winter

→ Activity Book 34

A Guessing Game

A Tiny Tot

⟶ Activity Book 36

A Noisy Nose

The Birthday Party

→ Activity Book 38

The Kangaroo

Activity Book 39

A Carrot, a Cookie, and a Cake

⟶ Activity Book 40

The Dog and the Duck

Purple

→ Activity Book 42

Run in the Rain

Activity Book 43

The Hungry Horse

⟶ Activity Book 44

The Yellow Bird

→ Activity Book 45

Vegetables

→ Activity Book 46

A Quick Quilt

The Zebra

➝ Activity Book 48

Activity Book 49

First, do Activity Book 50.

The Cat

The cat is on the mat.
The cat is fat.
The cat sees the fat bat.

First, do Activity Book 51.

A Cake

Cookie Monster wants a cake.
He can bake a cake.
He can take the cake to the lake.

First, do Activity Book 52.

Quack Quack

The duck is black.
Her sack is black.
It is on her back.
She goes quack, quack.

Quack.
Quack.

First, do Activity Book 53.

A Ball on the Wall

The ball is on the wall
She wants the ball.
Big Bird is tall.
He can see the ball.
Can he get the ball?

A Tan Van

The man wants a van.
He sees a van.
The van is tan.
The man can buy the tan van.

First, do Activity Book 55.

Don't Quit

Don't sit down!
Don't quit!
Hit the ball.

She hit the ball!

First, do Activity Book 56.

You Can Win

See that pin?
It's in his hand.
You can win.
You can win the pin.

First, do Activity Book 57.

A Fall

She fell down.
Her lip hurts.
Her hip hurts.
Her head hurts.
Can you see the rip?

First, do Activity Book 58.

Run

Run, Cookie Monster, run.
Run to get the bun.
It is fun to run.
It is fun to run in the sun.

First, do Activity Book 59.

Get the Bug

See the bug.
The bug is on the rug.

See the bug.
The bug is on the mug.
Get the bug!

First, do Activity Book 60.

Hop, Hop!

Hop! Hop!
Hop to the mop.
Hop to the top.
Don't pop the balloon!

First, do Activity Book 61.

The Hot Pot

Ernie got a new pot.
The pot got hot.
Do not touch the hot pot!

First, do Activity Book 62.

Get the Net

Get the net!
Get the net!
Let me have the net.
But don't get wet.

First, do Activity Book 63.

A Pen

Ten men see a pen.
The ten men all want the pen.
Can all ten men use one pen?

First, do Activity Book 64.

Let's

Let's sit on the wall.
Let's count the ten black bats.
Let's get wet. It's hot.
Let's pop the balloon with a pin.

Let's run in the sun.
Let's take the bug to the lake.
Let's pack the tan sack.
Let's take a sip.

Let's all run to Sesame Street!